Edited by
ANDREW ROBERTS
NEIL JOHNSON
and **TOM MILTON**

INTRODUCTORY GUIDE

The Bible Reading Fellowship
15 The Chambers, Vineyard
Abingdon OX14 3FE
brf.org.uk

The Bible Reading Fellowship (BRF) is a Registered Charity (233280)

ISBN 978 0 85746 677 8
First published 2018
Reprinted 2018
10 9 8 7 6 5 4 3 2 1

Acknowledgements
Unless otherwise acknowledged, scripture quotations from The New Revised Standard Version of the Bible, Anglicised edition, copyright © 1989, 1995 by the Division of Christian Education of the National Council of the Churches of Christ in the United States of America. Used by permission. All rights reserved.

Scripture quotations marked NJB are from The New Jerusalem Bible © 1985 by Darton, Longman & Todd Ltd and Doubleday, a division of Bantam Doubleday Dell Publishing Group, Inc.

Photograph on page 27 copyright © Thinkstock; photographs on pages 5, 6, 8, 13, 15, 17 and 19 copyright © Tom Milton and the Birmingham Methodist Circuit.

Every effort has been made to trace and contact copyright owners for material used in this resource. We apologise for any inadvertent omissions or errors, and would ask those concerned to contact us so that full acknowledgement can be made in the future.

A catalogue record for this book is available from the British Library

Printed and bound by CPI Group (UK) Ltd, Croydon CR0 4YY

CONTENTS

To order more copies of the Holy Habits resources, or to find out
how to download pages for printing or projection on screen,
please visit brfonline.org.uk/holy-habits.

WELCOME

Welcome to this Guide to Holy Habits. It has been exciting to see how Christians of all traditions have embraced the Holy Habits vision for a Spirit-filled life of discipleship that is holy, adventurous and missional.

These resources have been developed to support churches seeking to deepen and develop such discipleship through the intentional living of ten habitual practices seen in the life of the earliest church, as portrayed by Luke in Acts 2:42–47.

The biblical scholars C.K. Barrett and James Dunn both believe that this passage is instructive for those seeking to form healthy disciple-making communities. Commenting on it, Barrett says:

> Luke wished his readers to see what the life of the Christians was like in the apostolic period in order that they might imitate it… His story is not simply a series of biographies but the story of a community.
>
> C.K. Barrett, *Acts 1–14* (T&T Clark, 2004), p. 160

Dunn, meanwhile, argues:

> [Luke's] portrayal may be somewhat idealised. But anyone who is familiar with movements of enthusiastic spiritual renewal will recognise authentic notes: the enthusiasm of the members of the renewal group, with a sense of overflowing joy, desire to come together frequently, eating together and worshipping and including the readiness for unreserved commitment to one another in a shared common life.
>
> James Dunn, *The Acts of the Apostles* (Epworth, 1996), p. 34

It is the hope and prayer of those who have developed these resources that those using them will discover that same enthusiastic spiritual renewal as these ancient and yet ever-new Holy Habits are lived afresh in these days.

They devoted themselves to the apostles' teaching and fellowship, to the breaking of bread and the prayers. Awe came upon everyone, because many wonders and signs were being done by the apostles. All who believed were together and had all things in common; they would sell their possessions and goods and distribute the proceeds to all, as any had need. Day by day, as they spent much time together in the temple, they broke bread at home and ate their food with glad and generous hearts, praising God and having the goodwill of all the people. And day by day the Lord added to their number those who were being saved.

ACTS 2:42–47

ETHOS

The nature of the Holy Habits

It is important to be aware that the Holy Habits are not ends in themselves. They are not just ten fun things to study or do, although we hope you will have fun in exploring and living them. Rather, they are composite parts of a habitual holy way of living: a way of living 'day by day' (Acts 2:46–47), both personally wherever we are called to be, and a way of living when we gather and serve together through the community of disciples we know as church; a way of life that encourages growth in discipleship, the formation of new disciples and a fuller experience for others of the kingdom of God.

The relationship between the Holy Habits

In real life, the Holy Habits are not lived in isolation. They are interrelated, and often they are intertwined. The resources have been developed to allow the Holy Habits to be explored one at a time, but in practising them it is important to do so in an integrated or cumulative way, with each building on the others. In each booklet, you will find suggestions on how the habits relate to each other.

The origins of Holy Habits

Holy Habits has grown out of a study of Acts 2:42–47 by Methodist minister Andrew Roberts. This study was first published in the *Epworth Review* theological journal (Volume 36, Number 3, July 2009) and then evolved into his book *Holy Habits* (Malcolm Down Publishing, 2016).

The first set of Holy Habits Resources was developed by the Birmingham Methodist Circuit. Those resources have been adapted by a small group of people from the Methodist Church and the United Reformed Church to form the present version. While drawing on the rich discipleship heritage of these two traditions in particular, they are accessible and useful for all those seeking to follow Jesus.

For a list of those involved in developing the resources, please see the Credits list on p. 23 of this guide and at the end of each booklet.

The values of Holy Habits

Holy Habits have been shaped by an understanding of discipleship based on two principles:

- It is a response to the call of Jesus.
- We learn and grow as disciples (personally and collectively) as we follow the one who calls. The Greek New Testament word for disciple, *mathetes*, literally means one who learns *as* they follow.

Holy Habits encourages a living out of discipleship that is:

- centred on and inspired by the divine community of Father, Son and Holy Spirit
- nurtured in the community of the church through smaller and larger groups, and one-to-one relationships
- lived out in the whole of life: in work, rest and play
- missional, participating in the mission of God and always seeking the blessing of others
- creative, imaginative and contextual
- for all.

Preparing for Holy Habits

Luke was very deliberate in the way he wrote. He begins our core passage with four key words: 'They devoted themselves to'. If Holy Habits is to be a fruitful experience, then it will need the same kind of devotion that Luke points to in Acts 2. This is not a quick fix.

Later on in the Introductory Guide, you will find practical ideas on how to journey with these resources. Here, it is important to note the need to approach this adventure with the kind of devotion that has been a hallmark of all movements of enthusiastic spiritual renewal.

As you embark on your journey, you may wish to pray this prayer for the faithful practice of Holy Habits, which starts with a passage from Romans 5:4–5.

Endurance produces character, and character produces hope,
    and hope does not disappoint us…
Gracious and ever-loving God, we offer our lives to you.
Help us always to be open to your Spirit in our thoughts
    and feelings and actions.
Support us as we seek to learn more about those habits of the Christian life
    which, as we practise them, will form in us the character of Jesus
    by establishing us in the way of faith, hope and love.
Amen

PREPARING FOR HOLY HABITS

For Holy Habits to be used fruitfully, the following tips are offered for preparing to use the resources, drawing on the wisdom and experience gained from developing the resources in Birmingham.

Policy

Holy Habits aims for the renewal of churches, or the formation of fresh expressions of church, as disciple-forming communities. If this aim is to be realised, it is important that Holy Habits is integral to the life, policy and strategy of the church(es), not an esoteric extra for the enthusiastic few.

Discipleship

In preparing for Holy Habits, it is important to set it in the context of forming and deepening discipleship. To do this, it is important to explore the nature and aims of Christian discipleship in services, small groups, recommended reading and/or an envisioning event, to be clear about the sort of disciples you are seeking to nurture and grow. The first part of Andrew Roberts' *Holy Habits* (Malcolm Down Publishing, 2016) book provides material to help.

Timetable

It is recommended that Holy Habits runs over a two-year period, with a new habit being introduced for exploration every two months (with longer intervals where needed). Local customs, needs and opportunities may lead to a different timeframe being adopted. As noted earlier, it is important not to 'park' a habit at the end of each period but to keep practising it as new habits go on to be explored.

Experience has shown that a six-month preparation period beforehand and a major launch event or service are really helpful in getting underway with Holy Habits. A midway review, and a concluding celebration and review to consider what's next, are also recommended.

The order in which the habits are explored is a matter for local discernment and decision, and will be influenced by context, the time or season of the year and ecumenical factors.

If Holy Habits is being explored by a group of churches, additional thought will need to be given to timings. In particular, whether there is one designated Sunday when all the churches are introduced to a new habit.

Practicalities

1 Teams

To run Holy Habits, a small team will be needed to oversee it and to organise its launch and review. It is helpful if the team represents a cross-section of the church family. This is a good opportunity to release people (including ordained people) to pursue and share their particular passions.

Depending on how many churches or groups are working together, you may find that having a further small team for each habit is useful, to coordinate all of the activity for that particular habit.

Particular tasks of this team will be to ensure that the following activities are undertaken – either by themselves or others as appropriate:

- Read the material well in advance and introduce it to the church(es) and key people (e.g. leadership teams, preachers, worship leaders, children's workers, small group leaders).
- Be available to offer further ideas and resources.
- Gather stories, testimonies and pictures of the habit in action.
- Think through how the habit can continue to be integral to the life of the church and the individuals who are part of it on an ongoing basis.

2 Collaborations

If a group of churches are exploring the Holy Habits together, it may be helpful for smaller churches in particular to cluster together, to share planning and resources – or for a larger church to partner with a smaller one to share resources and ideas.

3 Budgets

There is no set budget for Holy Habits, but, noting Luke's comment that 'they devoted themselves', it will be helpful to make good resourcing a priority when church budgets are being set.

4 Support

Many churches and denominations have officers for whom deepening discipleship is part of their remit. Do consider inviting them to be part of your planning, exploring and reviewing of Holy Habits.

Launch

It is significant that Luke's portrayal of the church in Acts 2 follows on immediately from the outpouring of the Spirit at Pentecost. Arguably, that event launched the church.

Each of the places that developed and tested the first versions of the Holy Habits resources chose to have a significant launch event – all but one at Pentecost. These proved to be very significant occasions and moments of renewal in themselves – with hundreds gathering in one place.

Appendix 1 includes a short drama from the first Birmingham Holy Habits launch service, which you are welcome to use.

Review

One of the tasks of the oversight group will be to monitor and review the working of Holy Habits on an ongoing basis. In particular, we would recommend a larger review after introducing the first five habits, and after introducing the last one, with the 'final' review asking the important questions of how to continue nurturing and living out these habits.

Holy Habits is a way of life for all people, of all ages and of all abilities. In exploring and living Holy Habits, please be aware of issues of inclusion.

Safeguarding

For all those participating in Holy Habits, it is essential that good safeguarding policies and practices are followed. All churches should have these. If you have any doubts or queries in this area, consult your church leaders or safeguarding officer.

Food safety and dietary needs

Eating Together is proving to be a particularly popular Holy Habit. Sharing food and drink is also encouraged in many of the other habits. Take care to ensure that, whenever food and drink are served, they are served safely and food allergies are catered for.

All ages and abilities

Many of the resources offered in the Holy Habit booklets can be used by all age and all ability groups. Some have a particular focus or application. Material for children and young people is spread throughout the booklets. Resources particularly suitable for children and families are marked ♟ and for young people ☺.

There are many extra resources that can be particularly helpful for children and younger people. Denominational children's families and youth workers have a wealth of expertise in these.

Holy Habits is for the whole church, and the church includes those whose personal circumstances mean they cannot generally share in the life of a local congregation. Please see Appendix 2 for a reflection on contextualising Holy Habits for those who are housebound or in care homes.

THE RESOURCES

The nature of the resources

The Holy Habits resources have been designed to be a gift to those who use them; a gift to be used imaginatively, creatively and contextually, made alive by the breath of the Holy Spirit. They are very much thought-starter ideas, not a script to be slavishly adhered to or a master plan. They cannot and do not say or cover everything there is to say about the Holy Habits. So where you find gaps, please explore the riches of scripture, your tradition and your experience to craft further thinking, ideas and expressions of these habits to help these practices become ever more a part of down-to-earth holy living.

Each Holy Habit booklet has three sections:

1 **Understanding the habit**
Introductory material for services of worship and groups.

2 **Forming the habit**
Material to help individuals and churches make these Holy Habits a regular way of life, including:
   a stories that show how these habits are transformative
   b suggested practices for individuals and churches to make the habits habitual
   c review questions for churches.

3 **Going further with the habit**
Material and ideas to help people go deeper, including:
   a pieces of theological reflection
   b further practices to help deepen the habit
   c suggested films and new media pieces to watch, and books and poems to read
   d art and photographs to reflect upon.

The materials are in a mix of styles and pitched at different levels; this is intentional. Contributions have come from a wide variety of authors, including children and young people, and in editing them together we have tried to preserve different voices and flavours. The materials are also intended to be a feast of ideas from which you can select some that are appropriate to your context and learning styles.

The suggestions for 'Forming the habit' are divided into three sections: sometimes, often and occasionally. While we have given some suggested frequency (daily/ weekly, etc.), these guidelines are not meant to be prescriptive – do what works for your context.

Worship resources

The worship resources in the booklets are provided to help you introduce each Holy Habit in a service of worship. They are offered to help you plan your times of worship, not as a fully polished order of service. Please use whatever works, add your own material and resources and make it fit your context and culture.

Hymns and songs

Hymn and song suggestions are drawn mostly from the following resources, although many appear in other song and hymn books:

- **CH4** – Church Hymnary 4 (also known as Hymns of Glory Songs of Praise)
- **RS** – Rejoice and Sing
- **SoF** – Songs of Fellowship 6
- **StF** – Singing the Faith

There are also many seasonally appropriate hymns and songs you could use.

Don't forget that you can also use hymns and songs for meditation or reflection, rather than just singing.

Prayer

As you explore each habit, you are invited to explore different ways of praying. Each habit has a number of suggestions for how you might pray creatively as part of a corporate act of **Worship**. These ideas are to help you form and sustain the Holy Habit of **Prayer** while also understanding and forming that particular habit.

Where creative prayer ideas involve the use of fragrance or food, take care to consider the needs of those members of your congregations who might have breathing difficulties or special dietary needs including diabetes, food allergies or intolerances, eating disorders or other restrictions around food and drink.

Bible

Bible verses quoted are from the New Revised Standard Version (NRSV) unless otherwise stated.

Group materials and activities

The booklets contain a variety of materials for use in small groups, from full Bible studies and session plans to illustrative activities and games. Some will be more suitable for different age ranges or contexts than others – please choose materials appropriately.

FORMING THE HABIT

In each booklet you will find material to help people reflect on how the Holy Habits can become a way of life. The practices of journalling, storytelling and forming a rhythm of life are particularly encouraged. As part of your preparations for Holy Habits, it is recommended that people are introduced to these practices (again, denominational officers may well be able to help with this).

Journalling

Journalling is regularly reflecting on your experiences, thoughts and encounters with God and keeping a note of your reflections. Many keep a written journal, but it could be a journal using art, or using technology such as a vlog (video log). You are invited to keep a journal during your journey through Holy Habits. Find some time to reflect on what you have been experiencing. Some find it helpful to have a set time every day, while others prefer to pick up their journal when they have time. However you choose to journal, try to make it a regular practice in your day or week. Take the opportunity to look back over your journal as the weeks progress. It is a good way to see how you may have changed, or discern how God has spoken to you, or how the Holy Habits are influencing your life.

Sharing stories

Real-life stories of how people and communities have been changed by God's grace are inspiring and powerful. One of the joys to emerge from those who participated in the Birmingham Holy Habits adventure, and indeed many who have read the *Holy Habits* book by Andrew Roberts (Malcolm Down Publishing, 2016), has been the stories of blessing and transformation as individuals and churches have engaged afresh with the way of life that is nurtured by practising the habits. You will find stories of transformation to encourage and inspire you in each of the booklets. As you live this experience, be alert to the stories that arise within and around you and, with appropriate permission, share them to encourage others. Stories can be shared in many ways including:

- testimonies in group meetings or services
- written pieces in magazines
- photo montages
- blogs, vlogs, videos and/or social media pieces including tweets.

Remember always to get the permission of those whose stories you seek to share if they are not already in the public domain. Sometimes you may agree to anonymise the person(s) involved. Take care to reference any stories that you share from other sources and seek appropriate copyright permissions if applicable.

Forming a rhythm of life

In Acts 2:42–47, Luke twice uses the phrase 'day by day'. By doing so, he highlights how the Holy Habits were a way of life lived rhythmically. In recent years, there has been a rediscovery of the value of rules or rhythms of life: patterns of prayer and regular practice of the other Holy Habits that deepen our dwelling in Christ and equip us in our day-to-day lives as kingdom-focused missionary disciples in the various contexts that we serve.

Many rhythms of life are developed more fully to be rules of life that encapsulate commitment and incorporate values as well as practices. Pete Greig, the founder of the 24-7 prayer movement, suggests: 'A rule of life is a set of principles and practices we build into the rhythm of our daily lives, helping us to deepen our relationship with God and to serve him more faithfully' (Pete Greig, *The Vision and the Vow*, Kingsway, 2005).

Rhythms of life can be very simple. The Hebrew prophet Micah provides a famous early example:

> What does the Lord require of you but to do justice, and to love kindness, and to walk humbly with your God?
> MICAH 6:8

Rhythms and rules of life are chosen personally and freely, not imposed by an external authority. You may wish to encourage the development of local or personal rhythms or rules of life as you explore and seek to live out Holy Habits.

GOING FURTHER WITH THE HABIT

Using the arts and media resources

In the 'Going further with the habit' section of the materials, you will find suggested **films** and **new media pieces** to watch, **books** and **poems** to read, and **art** and **photographs** to reflect upon. To use these resources fruitfully, you may wish to form a film or book club. Guidance on how to form these is widely available online, and you could also ask denominational training officers for help. Take care to ensure that you comply with any copyright or licensing requirements.

With art and photographs, the images provided can be used in services or group meetings to introduce and help reflection upon the Holy Habits. You can download the images from **www.methodist.org.uk/artcollection**. You are also encouraged to have a go at developing your own images and pieces of work.

Sarah Middleton, a trustee of the Methodist Modern Art Collection (from which works are drawn throughout the Holy Habits series), offers some thoughts on engaging with art for theological reflection and deepening of discipleship, including thoughts on creating your own art, in Appendix 3.

CREDITS

The Holy Habits editorial/ development team:
Ben Clymo
Caz Hague
Deborah Humphries
Tricia Mitchell
Tony Moodie
Meg Prowting
Andrew Roberts
Stuart Scott

The Birmingham Holy Habits reference group:
Vicki Atkinson
Rachel Frank
Caz Hague
Deborah Humphries
Neil Johnson (Chair)
Tom Milton
Andrew Roberts
Michele Simms

Additional contributors:
Ian Adams
Gail Adcock
Sarah Middleton
Stephanie Neville
Pat Nimmo
Matthew Prevett
Kathryn Price
Kevin Snyman
Nick Stanyon
Sam Taylor
Fiona Thomas
Phil Wall
Andrew Wood

With thanks to Morse-Brown Design for their helpfulness and generosity in developing the original design style.

Please see individual booklets for other contributors to specific booklets.

p. 22: *Fool of God (Christ in the Garden)* and *The Dalit Madonna* from the Methodist Modern Art Collection, © TMCP, used with permission.

APPENDIX 1
A reflection on the Holy Habits

Person 1 needs to be seated at the front and not involved in the actions that take place in response to wonderings. The actions can be started by any willing participants (we have used young people in our churches), but it is hoped that all will join in.

Person 1: I wonder what it would be like to be part of a church like that. A church that embraced the roominess of God and so made room for others; a church that lives with an open hand and an open heart.

(Hold out hand and long pause.)

Person 1: I wonder what it would be like to be part of a church that ate together…

Person 2: Let's eat together. *(Share some appropriate food that all can eat.)*

Person 1: I wonder what it would be like to be part of a church that prayed together…

Person 2: *(Light a candle and place it on the table. Invite people to hold a minute's silence or insert your intercessory prayers.)*

Person 1: I wonder what it would be like to be part of a church that made more disciples…

Person 2: *(Flick people with water from a bowl using a heather or lavender sprig. You could explain that some churches use this to remind people of their baptismal vows.)*

Person 1: I wonder what it would be like to be part of a church that lived generously…

Person 2: *(Share handfuls of grapes around.)*

Person 1: I wonder what it would be like to be part of a church that broke bread together...

Person 2: *(Break a large gluten-free loaf high in the air and place it on the table, or distribute.)*

Person 1: I wonder what it would be like to be part of a church that served one another and their community...

Person 2: *(Wash the feet of one person in the congregation.)*

Person 1: I wonder what it would be like to be part of a church where everyone felt part of the fellowship...

Person 2: *(Link hands with those gathered and encourage others to do so.)*

Person 1: I wonder what it would be like to be part of a church that worshipped together...

Person 2: *(Sing a chorus of something well known and encourage others to join in, or place a symbol of worship on the table.)*

Person 1: I wonder what it would be like to be part of a church that studied the word of God together...

Person 2: *(Read a well-known passage or verse out loud from a Bible and place it on the table.)*

Person 1: I wonder what it would be like to be part of a church that shared all they had...

Person 2: *(Take the offering.)*

Person 1: Wouldn't it be good if the church embraced all those Holy Habits...

Person 3: *(Read out Acts 2:42–47.)*

Person 1: I want to be part of a church like that.

A reflection on Holy Habits for those who are in care homes or housebound

Care homes

The church in such homes is existing in an environment that has its own rhythms and life, focused around care. This often means that 'time apart' for any group, however small, is difficult to arrange and often interrupted. In addition, as physical and mental inhibitions are faced, along with a wide variety of Christian experience, the focus is better on one-to-one conversations. Group discussions are difficult to host. The ecumenical nature of the church in care homes is another factor to be borne in mind.

To explore Holy Habits, or at least some of them, will require imagination, the careful choice of material used and the building of personal relationships. Care homes are places of routine and those who struggle with memory loss or dementia find this positive. The idea of Holy Habits that are part of building and expressing faith would seem to have a 'natural fit'.

It is often assumed that the maintenance of 'cherished traditions' in people's spiritual lives is vital, but, as people face the challenges of failing physical and intellectual capacity, life changes radically and fresh ways of practising spiritual Holy Habits need to be explored sensitively. The use of images and sensory material, craft activities, etc. can come into their own and be more important here than in a traditional church setting.

Care homes present the challenge of relating to a broad spectrum of intellectual and physical capability (not necessarily absent in the church setting!) and this requires sensitivity. Failing sight is an obvious obstacle to Bible reading. So, simple Bible reading can be an individual or group activity in a care home. This might be straightforward reading, or include some opportunity for reflection. One consequence of spirituality in dementia is that we depend to an increasing degree on others and on the grace of God in our spiritual lives. In relation to Holy Habits, this would mean an increasing degree of enabling in a one-to-one relationship.

Housebound

For the elderly housebound, many of the observations relating to care homes may also apply. The existence of good personal relationships is clearly a prerequisite. In the private home setting, there may well be opportunity for a broader engagement with Holy Habits, particularly if the individual involved is happy for a small group to gather in their home. There are clear sensitivities to observe in this setting.

The relationship between 'habits' and 'routine' is probably as important here as in a care home setting. It would be important for the host to be clear about details such as dates and time, number of sessions, etc. Those visiting would need to be sensitive to changes in circumstances for the host, such as health, carers attending, etc. There are particular sensitivities around meeting in a person's 'private space' with an awareness of when it may be appropriate to leave.

APPENDIX 3
Art and worship

In medieval times, artists and makers presented the story of Christian salvation in stained glass, carvings and wall paintings. In recent times, many adults have felt less confident engaging with a piece of art than with the written word. Their own school experience may even have convinced them that they were no good at art. Today, the educational curriculum includes 'looking skills'.

Visual literacy (the technical term) is a pathway that takes us beyond the first apprehension of a work of art. It involves being able to create meaning from visual images. Much of what we experience and process as part of being human (the past, the future, our memories, our expectations) we do not physically see at the moment of dealing with it. Yet, these are realities. Some of us are able to visualise with 'the mind's eye' more easily than others. Artists use their skills and imagination to create a bridge between the material world and the invisible realities. Jesus Christ, God incarnate, was doing this continually in his ministry on earth, through his parables and word pictures: 'I am the bread of life', 'The kingdom of heaven is like a mustard seed', 'Consider the lilies of the field'. How important it is that the church harnesses again the skills of looking – looking with the inner eye as well as the outer eye.

How then might we open ourselves up to an encounter with the Holy Spirit when viewing a work of art?

Here are a few starters:

- Consider the subject matter – what do you know of the cultural context in which the image was created and exists?
- Are any symbols being used – and how do you interpret these? Be aware that symbols can convey different meanings to different cultural groups.
- What is the medium (for example, paint, wood, clay, etc.) and in what way does the medium enhance the message? This is an important question, especially concerning reproductions, where the texture, size and shape of the original may not be immediately apparent.
- Can you define the 'feel' of the image?

It has been said that great civilisations are remembered not for their economic successes but by the art they leave behind. Art can celebrate, calm, exhilarate and

The Supper at Emmaus, Ceri Richards (1903–71).
From the Methodist Modern Art Collection, © TMCP, used with permission.

challenge. The way people decipher meaning in a work of art depends upon their educational, social and religious backgrounds. We do well to remember this as we reflect theologically, while believing that the risen Jesus transcends time and space and culture.

In his letter to the church at Ephesus, Paul describes human beings as 'God's work of art, created in Christ Jesus for the good works which God has already designated to make up our way of life' (Ephesians 2:10, NJB). What a splendid metaphor for our discipleship!

An encounter with a painting, a sculpture or other piece of visual art can help us to become more Christ-like. The art acts as a mirror. By looking into this mirror, we can see deep inside of ourselves, see what motivates and moves us, see what might need changing. The lyrics of Michael Jackson's 'Man in the Mirror' reflect upon this.

If it is not already your practice, it is hoped that you will find it enriching to dwell on a work of art as part of your prayer life. See where your observation and meditation take you. Have some brushes handy, and that may mean your mobile device or tablet – there are various 'sketchbook' apps!

978 0 85746 678 5, 64 pages

978 0 85746 679 2, 64 pages

978 0 85746 680 8, 64 pages

978 0 85746 681 5, 64 pages

978 0 85746 682 2, 64 pages

978 0 85746 683 9, 64 pages

'To understand the disciplines of the Christian life without practising them habitually is like owning a fine collection of soap but never having a wash. The team behind Holy Habits knows this, which is why they have produced these excellent and practical resources. Use them, and by God's grace you will grow in holiness.'

Paul Bayes, Bishop of Liverpool

978 0 85746 684 6, 64 pages

978 0 85746 685 3, 64 pages

978 0 85746 686 0, 64 pages

978 0 85746 687 7, 64 pages

Looking for enough resources to use with your Holy Habits team? Order a CHURCH PACK and get five copies of each of the habits for £199.60 (save 20%)

Go to brfonline.org.uk/holy-habits to order now

'This set of ten resources will enable churches and individuals to begin to establish "habits of faithfulness". In the United Reformed Church, we are calling this process of developing discipleship, "Walking the Way: Living the life of Jesus today" and I have no doubt that this comprehensive set of resources will enable us to do just that.'
Revd Richard Church, Deputy General Secretary (Discipleship), United Reformed Church

'Here are some varied and rich resources to help further deepen our discipleship of Christ, encouraging and enabling us to adopt the life-transforming habits that make for following Jesus.'
Revd Dr Martyn Atkins, Team Leader & Superintendent Minister, Methodist Central Hall, Westminster

'The Holy Habits resources will help you, your church, your fellowship group, to engage in a journey of discovery about what it really means to be a disciple today. I know you will be encouraged, challenged and inspired as you read and work your way through each chapter. There is lots to study together and pray about, and that can only be good as our churches today seek to bring about the kingdom of God.'
Revd Loraine Mellor, President of the Methodist Conference 2017/18

'The Holy Habits resources help weave the spiritual through everyday life. They're a great tool that just get better with use. They help us grow in our desire to follow Jesus as their concern is formation not simply information.'
Olive Fleming Drane and John Drane

'The Holy Habits resources are an insightful and comprehensive manual for living in the way of Jesus in the 21st century: an imaginative, faithful and practical gift for the church that will sustain and invigorate our life and mission in a demanding world. The Holy Habits resources are potentially transformational for a church.'
Revd Ian Adams, Mission Spirituality Adviser for Church Mission Society

'The Holy Habits resources are a rich mine of activities for all ages to help change minds, attitudes and behaviours. I love the way many different people groups are represented and celebrated, and the constant references to the complex realities of 21st-century life.'
Lucy Moore, Founder of BRF's Messy Church